30 Days To Speak It Into Reality

30 DAYS TO SPEAK IT INTO REALITY

A Goal Manifestation Journey

ELIZABETH MOORE

Copyright © 2025 by Elizabeth Moore

All rights reserved.

No part of this publication may be reproduced, stored in a retrieval system, or transmitted in any form or by any means—electronic, mechanical, photocopying, recording, or otherwise—without the prior written permission of the author, except for brief quotations used in reviews, articles, or scholarly works.

This book is intended to provide inspiration and guidance based on personal experience and belief. The author makes no guarantees regarding the outcome of applying the ideas discussed. Readers are encouraged to use their own judgment and discretion.

For permissions or inquiries, please contact:
read.moore.books25@gmail.com

Published by Kindle Direct Publishing (KDP)
Printed in the United States of America
First Edition

ISBN: 979-8-218-69895-9

Cover design by Joshua Stewart

Your voice is not just sound—it is creation. Speak with clarity. Speak with courage. Speak, and let your life rise to meet your words.

Introduction

Welcome to *30 Days to Speak It Into Reality.* This isn't just a book—it's an invitation. A sacred space to come home to your voice, your vision, and your power. Whether you've manifested before or this is your first journey inward, I want you to know one thing: there is no rush.

This process is not meant to be hurried. It's not a sprint. It's not about "fixing" your life overnight. It's about becoming more present with who you already are, one spoken word at a time.

Each day of this journey is designed to bring you back to the now. Because the now is where your power lives. The now is where your future begins. When you slow down and engage with the daily practices—speaking, journaling, reflecting—you begin to align with your truth in a way that sticks.

Some days will feel light and easy. Others might stir something deeper. All of it is welcome. There is no right way to go through this book—only *your* way. Be gentle with yourself. Be honest. Be willing to show up fully, even if it's messy.

Speak each affirmation with your whole heart. Reflect on the journal prompts without judgment. Trust that each small step is rewiring your belief system and reconnecting you with your highest self.

You don't have to get it perfect. You just have to get present.

Let this journey unfold. Let it be sacred. Let it be yours.

Now take a breath, take your time, and begin.

The Power of the Spoken Word

Why speaking intentions works

Words are more than just sounds—they are frequencies, vibrations, and declarations that shape reality. When you speak something with belief, emotion, and repetition, you begin to energetically align yourself with that outcome. The spoken word is one of the most direct ways to engage your subconscious mind and set your frequency to attract what you desire.

In spiritual teachings, the power of the word is sacred. From biblical scripture to ancient mantras, speaking aloud has always been a tool for creation. When you speak with intention, you activate both spiritual law and psychological priming. You begin to move, act, and feel in alignment with your spoken desires.

Real-world and spiritual principles
On a practical level, speaking out loud can solidify goals, improve clarity, and increase self-accountability. Spiritually, your voice is a divine instrument of creation. What you say, you send. What you repeat, you reinforce. Speaking is the bridge between the invisible (thought) and the visible (reality).

When you declare, "I am abundant," you're not just affirming a wish—you're creating a reality.

Preparing Your Inner Space

Clearing resistance and aligning with your why

Before you begin speaking your desires into reality, you must make space for them. This means clearing out limiting beliefs, fears, or internal resistance that may block your voice. What parts of you still feel unworthy of asking? What old stories are you still rehearsing?

Alignment begins with honesty. What do you really want? And why do you want it? Your 'why' is your fuel. The clearer and more rooted it is, the stronger your manifestations will be.

Daily practices that support manifestation

To support your journey:

- Begin each day with breathwork or meditation to quiet inner noise.
- Speak affirmations aloud with emotion and clarity.
- Journal to process resistance and reinforce belief.
- Visualize yourself already living the life you are speaking into being.

Your inner world sets the tone for everything you create. When it's grounded, clear, and receptive—your words become unstoppable.

You are the vessel. Prepare it with care.

The Journey Begins ...

Day 1 – I Declare My Vision

Affirmation: "I speak my vision with clarity and conviction."

Everything begins with a clear declaration. Today, you choose to speak your desires aloud—not as a wish, but as a commitment. When you speak your vision, you give it life.

Say it boldly: "I am ready to manifest what I desire." This is the day you stop playing small with your dreams. Your voice is a tool of creation.

Let your vision be heard by the Universe. Let it echo through your body, your choices, your energy. You are the narrator of your reality—start telling a powerful story.

Journal Prompt:

- What is the vision I am ready to manifest?
- How does it feel to speak it aloud with confidence?
- What is one bold statement I can say today to claim it?

Speak your vision. It's the beginning of everything.

Day 2 – I Am Worthy of My Desires

Affirmation: "I am inherently worthy of everything I desire."

You don't have to earn your worth. You are already worthy. Today, release the lie that you need to struggle, prove, or wait to deserve your desires.

Speak this aloud: "I am enough. I am deserving. I am ready."

Worthiness is a frequency. When you speak from that place, you become a magnet for miracles. Your voice becomes an affirmation of who you truly are.

Journal Prompt:

- Where have I been questioning my worthiness?
- How can I affirm my worth with my words today?
- What changes when I believe I am enough right now?

Speak worthiness. You are already whole.

Day 3 – I Speak What I Want (Not What I Fear)

Affirmation: "My words are rooted in desire, not fear."

Most people speak more about what they don't want than what they do. Today, shift that pattern. Your language is a mirror of your focus.

Catch yourself in real time. When you hear fear, flip it into desire.

Instead of "I don't want to be broke," say, "I welcome abundance."

Instead of "I'm afraid of being alone," say, "I attract love and connection."

Let your voice become a map toward what you want—not a spotlight on what you fear.

Journal Prompt:

- What fears have been dominating my speech?
- How can I reframe them into empowered desires?
- What new phrases will I use starting today?

Speak from desire. You're always listening.

Day 4 – I Claim My Identity

Affirmation: "I speak as the version of me who already has it."

Manifestation isn't about waiting—it's about becoming. Today, you speak from your future self.

Ask: How does the version of me who already has it speak?

Use "I am" statements with boldness:

- I am successful.
- I am radiant.
- I am attracting aligned blessings.

This is not pretending. It's preparing. You're tuning your energy to the frequency of fulfillment.

Journal Prompt:

- Who is the version of me that already has what I want?
- What does that version believe and say?
- How can I speak from that identity today?

Speak as them. They are already within you.

Day 5 – I Align My Energy

Affirmation: "My words, thoughts, and actions align with my vision."

Alignment is where power lives. You can't speak abundance while thinking lack and expecting flow. Today, check in: Are my words in harmony with what I want?

Let your language reflect alignment. Speak from certainty. Speak from clarity. Speak from the place that already believes.

Alignment amplifies manifestation. When your voice, thoughts, and energy agree, the Universe listens.

Journal Prompt:

- Where have I been misaligned in my words or energy?
- What new aligned phrase will I repeat today?
- How can I better embody my vision?

Speak aligned. Let your life follow.

Day 6 – I Speak From Belief

Affirmation: "My words are grounded in unshakable belief."

Belief is the fuel of manifestation. Today, you root your speech in knowing—not hoping, not doubting, but knowing. Speak with the energy of "it's already mine."

Instead of saying, "I hope I get the opportunity," say, "I am preparing for the opportunity that is already on its way."

Let your language reflect inner certainty. Speak like someone who knows the outcome is inevitable.

Journal Prompt:

- Where have I been speaking from doubt?
- How can I strengthen my belief through my words?
- What's one powerful belief statement I will use today?

Speak belief. It builds your world.

Day 7 – I Invite Miracles

Affirmation: "I speak as one aligned with magic and miracles."

The miraculous becomes normal when you make space for it. Today, invite the extraordinary into your ordinary moments.

Speak openness. Speak magic. Say, "I am open to being surprised by joy."

Let the unexpected become welcome. Speak like someone who trusts that unseen support is already in motion.

Journal Prompt:

- How do I define a miracle?
- When was the last time I experienced the unexpected in a good way?
- What can I say today to invite magic into my life?

Speak wonder. The Universe is listening.

Day 8 – I Detach With Grace

Affirmation: "I speak desire without demanding outcomes."

Desire is powerful. But clinging? That blocks flow. Today, practice speaking your vision while releasing attachment to how and when it arrives.

Say, "This or something better." Say, "I trust what's for me will find me."

You don't have to force. You don't have to chase. Just speak and release. Detachment is not indifference—it's trust in motion.

Journal Prompt:

- Where am I gripping too tightly to outcomes?
- How can I soften my language around timing and control?
- What would it feel like to speak from complete trust?

Speak and release. Let grace carry it.

Day 9 – I Create With My Voice

Affirmation: "Every word I speak builds my reality."

Words are not empty. They are instructions. Today, become more intentional with the energy behind your voice.

Speak beauty. Speak clarity. Speak wholeness.

Catch the unconscious phrases that no longer serve you and choose something better. Don't just react—create.

Journal Prompt:

- What words do I say often that I want to release?
- What new phrases align with my truth and power?
- How can I be more creative and intentional with my voice today?

Speak with purpose. You are creating with every word.

Day 10 – I Am a Magnet for Good

Affirmation: "Goodness finds me because I speak it."

Your words set the tone for what shows up. Today, speak the frequency of "already blessed." Not waiting—receiving.

Say things like, "I always attract the right people." Say, "Something beautiful is unfolding right now."

Speak as if you are already living the life you asked for—and watch how the world begins to echo you.

Journal Prompt:

- What does it mean for me to be a magnet for good?
- What affirmations make me feel more open to receiving?
- How can I express gratitude in advance with my words?

Speak gratitude. Watch your life reflect it.

Day 11 – I Tune Inward

Affirmation: "I listen to the wisdom within."

Before you speak outwardly, listen inwardly. Today, you quiet the noise and return to your own knowing. The most powerful words come from deep connection to self.

Silence isn't empty—it's full of guidance. Speak only what aligns with your truth.

Ask yourself, "Is this my voice or someone else's?" Let your words be an authentic reflection of your soul.

Journal Prompt:

- When do I feel most connected to my inner voice?
- What truth has been whispering to me?
- How can I honor my inner wisdom in my speech today?

Speak from within. That's where your power lives.

Day 12 – I Release Doubt

Affirmation: "I let go of doubt and trust in my divine path."

Doubt is a natural visitor, but it doesn't have to be a permanent resident. When you entertain doubt, you water the weeds of fear. But when you speak trust, you make space for confidence to grow.

Today's intention is to recognize where doubt lingers and replace it with faith. You don't need all the answers—you just need the courage to believe that your words, actions, and energy are enough to move mountains.

Doubt whispers, but your voice roars. Speak your belief louder than your fear. Speak life into your journey.

Journal Prompt:

- What doubts have been holding me back?
- What truths can I affirm to replace those doubts?
- How does it feel to speak from a place of unwavering trust?

Speak belief. Doubt cannot dwell where faith lives.

Day 13 – I Embody My Future Self

Affirmation: "I am already the person I am becoming."

Manifestation is not just about attracting something new—it's about becoming someone new. Today's practice is about embodiment: walking, talking, thinking, and speaking as the version of you who already has what you desire.

Ask yourself: How would my future self show up today? How would they speak? What would they believe?

When you embody the future, you collapse the timeline between where you are and where you're going. Step into that energy. Speak as if it is already yours—because it is.

Journal Prompt:

- Who is the version of me that has already manifested my desire?
- What habits, beliefs, and language does that version live by?
- How can I start embodying that identity today?

Speak from your future. Become it now.

Day 14 – I Stay in High Vibration

Affirmation: "My energy is my magnet. I protect and elevate my vibration."

Your vibration is your frequency, and your frequency is your invitation. When you stay in a high vibration—love, joy, gratitude, peace—you attract more of the same.

Staying in high vibration doesn't mean ignoring hard feelings; it means choosing to return to your power again and again. Speak words that lift. Surround yourself with beauty. Take actions that energize. Let your life become a broadcast of light.

Today, let your voice be a tuning fork for your frequency. Speak from joy. Speak with love. Speak into elevation.

Journal Prompt:

- What raises my vibration instantly?
- What drains my energy, and how can I limit or transform it?
- What words or phrases can I speak today to maintain a high frequency?

Speak light. Your energy is your invitation.

Day 15 – I Detach from the Outcome

Affirmation: "I surrender the outcome and trust the unfolding."

Attachment can be a form of control in disguise. When we cling too tightly to how something should happen, we block the infinite ways it *could* happen. Detachment doesn't mean giving up—it means giving over.

Today, speak release. Say aloud, "I trust that what's meant for me will find me in the perfect time and way." This opens the flow. It allows miracles, surprise, and divine timing to take center stage.

Speak your desire—then release the need to chase it. The more you let go, the more you allow.

Journal Prompt:

- What outcome am I currently holding too tightly?
- How can I release control while staying aligned with my vision?
- What would it feel like to fully surrender the 'how' and 'when'?

Speak surrender. Let the magic unfold.

Day 16 – I Invite Joy In

Affirmation: "Joy is welcome here. I make space for happiness."

Joy is not a reward; it's a right. It's not something you earn by completing your to-do list or checking off goals. Joy is a vibration that fuels manifestation—and today, you are consciously choosing to let it in.

Look for joy in simple moments: sunlight, laughter, music, movement, connection. Speak joy aloud. Say, "I choose joy today," and let it ripple through your being. The more you welcome it, the more it finds you.

You don't have to wait for joy. Invite it. Receive it. Speak it.

Journal Prompt:

- What brings me pure, unfiltered joy?
- Where have I been postponing joy, and why?
- How can I infuse joy into my words, choices, and day?

Speak joy. Let it live in you.

Day 17 – I Own My Power

Affirmation: "I own my voice, my truth, and my power."

You are powerful—not because of anything external, but because of who you are at your core. Today is about claiming your inner authority. No more shrinking. No more playing small.

Speak from your full self. Own your worth. Take up space in the room, the relationship, the dream. Your power is not arrogance—it's alignment. When you own it, you give others permission to do the same.

This is not the day to whisper. This is the day to declare.

Journal Prompt:

- Where have I been giving away my power?
- What does it look and feel like when I stand fully in my truth?
- How will I speak and act differently when I own my power?

Speak boldly. You are the force you've been waiting for.

Day 18 – I Choose Peace

Affirmation: "Peace is my power. I choose calm over chaos."

In a noisy world, peace is a revolution. It is not the absence of challenge, but the presence of clarity and inner stillness. Today, you are choosing peace—not because everything is perfect, but because your spirit deserves rest.

Speak peace into your thoughts. Speak it into your environment. Be the calming presence in the room, the relationship, the moment.

You manifest faster from peace than you ever will from panic. Your calm is a magnet. Let peace be your anchor today.

Journal Prompt:

- What disrupts my peace, and how can I shift it?
- What rituals help me return to calm?
- How can I speak peace into today, no matter what comes?

Speak peace. Let it ripple outward.

Day 19 – I Celebrate the Journey

Affirmation: "I honor how far I've come and trust where I'm going."

Manifestation isn't just about the destination—it's about the evolution. Every step, every detour, every delay has shaped you. Today, take a moment to pause and celebrate the journey.

Celebrate your growth, your resilience, your progress. Speak gratitude over your path. Acknowledge what you've overcome, what you've learned, and how you've expanded. Let celebration be part of your vibration.

You are further than you think and stronger than you know.

Journal Prompt:

- What milestones have I reached that deserve to be celebrated?
- How have I grown in the past 19 days?
- What can I honor about myself right now?

Speak celebration. You are becoming.

Day 20 – I Expand My Capacity to Receive

Affirmation: "I open wide to receive all the good life has for me."

Manifestation requires more than desire—it requires readiness. Sometimes the only thing standing between you and your blessings is your ability to receive them.

Today, stretch your receiving muscle. Speak aloud, "I am open to receive with ease, grace, and gratitude." Release guilt. Let go of the belief that you must earn or struggle for what you want.

You are worthy of overflow. Make room for it with your voice, your heart, and your energy.

Journal Prompt:

- Where in my life am I blocking my own blessings?
- What does it feel like to be fully open to receiving?
- How can I expand my receiving capacity today?

Speak yes. Let it pour in.

Day 21 – I Release the Need to Rush

Affirmation: "I let go of urgency. I trust divine timing."

Rushing creates resistance. It sends a signal to the Universe that you don't believe your manifestation is on the way. Today, release the pressure to hurry. Breathe deeply into the now.

When you let go of urgency, you make space for patience, presence, and peace. Trust that everything you desire is already making its way to you. There is no need to chase what's already yours.

Speak slowly. Move intentionally. Allow the journey to unfold.

Journal Prompt:

- Where in my life am I rushing, and why?
- What am I afraid will happen if I slow down?
- How can I trust the timing of my manifestation today?

Speak ease. Your timeline is sacred.

Day 22 – I Attract Aligned Opportunities

Affirmation: "I attract what aligns with my purpose and power."

When you are clear, grounded, and intentional, the Universe responds. Opportunities begin to appear—ones that match not just your desire, but your readiness.

Today, speak alignment. Say, "I attract only what supports my highest path." This is a declaration of self-trust and discernment. You don't need just *any* opportunity—you need the *right* ones. And they are already being drawn to your energy.

Stay open, stay intentional, stay expectant. What's meant for you will recognize you.

Journal Prompt:

- What does an aligned opportunity feel like to me?
- How can I recognize what is aligned versus what is a distraction?
- What kind of opportunities am I calling in right now?

Speak alignment. Let the right doors open.

Day 23 – I Radiate Confidence

Affirmation: "I move through life with bold, grounded confidence."

Confidence is magnetic. It signals to the world—and to yourself—that you are ready, capable, and deserving. When you radiate confidence, you activate your power to manifest.

Confidence isn't about pretending or perfection. It's about knowing who you are and speaking from that place of certainty. Today, practice affirming your strength out loud. Let your words reflect belief in your value, your vision, and your voice.

Stand tall. Speak clearly. Move boldly.

Journal Prompt:

- What makes me feel most confident in myself?
- Where in my life could I use more confidence right now?
- What would I say or do today if I fully believed in myself?

Speak boldly. You are your own evidence.

Day 24 – I Honor My Desires

Affirmation: "My desires are divine. I honor what I want without shame."

Your desires are not random—they are sacred messages from your soul. When you ignore or downplay what you want, you disconnect from your truth. Today, you will honor your desires without apology.

Say it out loud: "What I want matters. What I want is worthy." This declaration rewires any old programming that told you to settle or suppress. Your desires were placed in your heart for a reason. Trust them. Nourish them. Speak them into existence.

Journal Prompt:

- What desire have I been afraid to admit or pursue?
- What would change if I fully honored that desire?
- How can I give my desire more voice and space today?

Speak truth. Your desires are divine instructions.

Day 25 – I Speak from Love, Not Fear

Affirmation: "I speak with love, clarity, and intention."

Fear tries to silence or distort your voice. It leads to withholding, over-explaining, shrinking, or attacking. Love, however, brings out your clearest truth. When you speak from love, you speak from power.

Today, choose words rooted in compassion, honesty, and courage. Whether you're speaking to yourself or others, pause and ask: Is this fear talking—or love?

Love doesn't mean weakness. It means integrity. Let your words uplift, heal, and affirm.

Journal Prompt:

- What does it sound like when I speak from fear?
- What shifts when I speak from love instead?
- Where in my life can I use more loving language—toward myself or others?

Speak love. It always echoes back.

Day 26 – I Welcome Support

Affirmation: "I am supported, seen, and surrounded by help."

Manifestation is not a solo mission. The Universe works through people, resources, conversations, and community. Today is about letting go of the myth that you have to do it all alone.

Speak your willingness to receive support: "I allow others to help me. I welcome divine connections." You are not weak for needing help. You are wise for receiving it.

Support may come from unexpected places. Be open. Speak it. Let it in.

Journal Prompt:

- Where in my life could I use more support?
- What has been holding me back from asking for or accepting help?
- How can I practice receiving support today?

Speak openness. You are never alone.

Day 27 – I Lead with Intention

Affirmation: "I lead my life with clear vision and mindful action."

Leadership is not about titles—it's about energy. It's about owning the direction of your life and choosing to act with purpose. Today, you are the leader of your reality.

Speak your vision. Make decisions from alignment. Lead with clarity and integrity in even the smallest choices. The more intentional you are, the more powerful your manifestation becomes.

Say it: "I lead my life on purpose."

Journal Prompt:

- What area of my life needs more intentional leadership?
- What does it look like to lead with clarity and care?
- How can I show up as a leader in my own life today?

Speak direction. You are guiding your future.

Day 28 – I Witness My Growth

Affirmation: "I honor the progress I've made and the person I've become."

Transformation often happens quietly. Day by day, shift by shift, you become more of who you truly are. Today, you pause to witness your growth—not just the external wins, but the internal evolution.

Speak appreciation for the version of you who kept going. Celebrate the wisdom you've gained, the strength you've discovered, and the alignment you've cultivated.

You are blooming—and your voice helped you grow.

Journal Prompt:

- In what ways have I grown over the past month?
- What qualities in myself am I most proud of right now?
- How can I continue to honor and nurture this growth?

Speak reflection. You are becoming your highest self.

Day 29 – I Anchor Into Faith

Affirmation: "I am grounded in faith. I trust what I cannot yet see."

Faith is the foundation of manifestation. It holds you steady in the waiting, fuels your vision, and anchors you through uncertainty. Today, you will strengthen your connection to faith—not blind belief, but rooted trust.

Say it aloud: "I believe it's already mine. I trust the path unfolding." Even if you don't yet see the outcome, you can still stand in certainty.

Let your voice be the bridge between your desire and its arrival.

Journal Prompt:

- What does faith feel like in my body, mind, and spirit?
- Where am I being invited to trust more deeply?
- What can I affirm today to anchor myself in belief?

Speak faith. Your belief builds the bridge.

Day 30 – I Speak It Into Reality

Affirmation: "I speak, I believe, and I receive."

You've come full circle—from desire to declaration, from silence to power, from hope to embodiment. Today is a celebration of your voice and the life it is shaping.

Speak your desires one more time—clearly, boldly, as if they're already here. Let the energy of completion wrap around your words. You are no longer someone who hopes. You are someone who speaks it into being.

This is your reality. Say it. Believe it. Live it.

Journal Prompt:

- What do I now feel empowered to speak into reality?
- How has my voice shifted over the past 30 days?
- What will I continue to affirm and embody moving forward?

Speak it. It is already becoming.

What Comes Next?

How to keep momentum beyond 30 days
Finishing this 30-day journey is just the beginning. You've activated your voice, clarified your desires, and aligned your energy—now it's about keeping the flame alive. Momentum doesn't mean constant action; it means staying connected to your intention, even in stillness.

Create space each week to revisit your affirmations. Speak them into your mornings. Reflect on what you've learned. Keep using your voice as a tuning fork for your truth.

Sustaining intention and growth
The key to lasting manifestation is consistency. That doesn't mean doing it perfectly—it means returning to your practice with love. Create rituals that remind you of your power. Surround yourself with words, music, people, and environments that keep you aligned.

Your journey evolves, and so does your voice. Keep speaking, even when you're uncertain. Especially when you're uncertain. That's when the magic deepens.

Your Manifestation Blueprint

Reviewing what worked
Pause and reflect: What affirmations spoke loudest to your spirit? What practices helped you stay grounded? Where did you feel the most transformation?

These reflections are gold. Use them to build a blueprint—a personal system that supports you every time you set a new goal or begin a new season.

Creating a repeatable system for future goals
To craft your blueprint:

- Identify your favorite affirmations and save them where you can access them daily.
- Note which journaling prompts opened breakthroughs and use them again.
- Choose 1–3 rituals that helped you feel most empowered.

Every time you want to manifest something new, return to this structure. Adapt it. Personalize it. Let it evolve with you.

Your voice is your compass. Now that you've spoken it into reality—keep speaking. Keep creating. Keep becoming.

Affirmations at a glance-

"I speak my vision with clarity and conviction."

"I am inherently worthy of everything I desire."

"My words are rooted in desire, not fear."

"I speak as the version of me who already has it."

"My words, thoughts, and actions align with my vision."

"My words are grounded in unshakable belief."

"I speak as one aligned with magic and miracles."

"I speak desire without demanding outcomes."

"Every word I speak builds my reality."

"Goodness finds me because I speak it."

"I listen to the wisdom within."

"I let go of doubt and trust in my divine path."

"I am already the person I am becoming."

"My energy is my magnet. I protect and elevate my vibration."

"I surrender the outcome and trust the unfolding."

"Joy is welcome here. I make space for happiness."

"I own my voice, my truth, and my power."

"Peace is my power. I choose calm over chaos."

"I honor how far I've come and trust where I'm going."

"I open wide to receive all the good life has for me."

"I let go of urgency. I trust divine timing."

"I attract what aligns with my purpose and power."

"I move through life with bold, grounded confidence."

"My desires are divine. I honor what I want without shame."

"I speak with love, clarity, and intention."

"I am supported, seen, and surrounded by help."

"I lead my life with clear vision and mindful action."

"I honor the progress I've made and the person I've become."

"I am grounded in faith. I trust what I cannot yet see."

"I speak, I believe, and I receive."

About the Author

Elizabeth Moore is a creative and purpose-driven soul who believes in the transformative power of words. She created this guide to help others find clarity, courage, and confidence by simply speaking their goals out loud. Her work blends intention, practicality, and a touch of magic to empower readers to live out loud.

Made in the USA
Columbia, SC
19 June 2025

0a9dabb2-92bd-4810-a0e6-12d567e0d4ffR01